D1297831

The Search for a Northern Route

Peter Chrisp

Thomson Learning
New York

Exploration & Encounters
The Search for the East
Voyages to the New World
The Spanish Conquests in the New World
The Search for a Northern Route

Cover pictures: Ptolemy's world map, recreated in 1486; and part of a sixteenth-century map showing Jacques Cartier in Canada.
Title page picture: Dutch ships sailing north in 1596, hoping to reach Asia.

First published in the United States in 1993 by
Thomson Learning
115 Fifth Avenue
New York, NY 10003

First published in 1993 by Wayland (Publishers) Ltd.

Library of Congress Cataloging-in-Publication Data
Chrisp, Peter.
 The search for a northern route / Peter Chrisp.
     p.   cm. — (Exploration & encounters, 1450–1550)
 Includes bibliographical references and index.
 ISBN 1-56847-122-X : $14.95
 1. Northwest Passage — Juvenile literature. 2. North America — Discovery and exploration — Juvenile literature. [1. Northwest Passage. 2. America — Discovery and exploration.] I. Title. II. Series.
G640.C47   1993
910'.9163'27 — dc20   93-30920

Printed in Italy

Picture acknowledgments
The publishers would like to thank the following for permission to use their pictures in this book: Archiv für Kunst und Geschichte, Berlin, *main cover picture, title page*, 5 (both), 12, 19, 29, 35, 36 (bottom), 38, 40, 45 (top); The Bridgeman Art Library 7, 15, 25, 26 (bottom), 31 (both), 36 (top), 39, 43; E. T. Archive 10 (top), 11, 24 (top), 26 (top), 27, 30, 33 (top); Mary Evans 4, 6 (bottom), 13 (top), 14, 16, 17 (bottom), 21, 22 (bottom), 34, 37, 42 (bottom); Eye Ubiquitous/Helene Rogers/TRIP 33 (bottom); Michael Holford *cover* (map); Peter Newark's Pictures 45 (bottom); PHOTRI 8, 10 (bottom), 32, 41, 42 (top); John Massey Stewart 20; Wayland Picture Library 6 (top), 17 (top), 23, 28. The artwork was supplied by Mike Taylor.

SOURCES OF QUOTES
For the sake of clarity, some minor changes have been made to the quotations, such as the substitution of modern words for sixteenth-century expressions.
Page 4: C. W. R. D. Moseley (trans.), *The Travels of Sir John Mandeville* (Penguin, 1983), p. 143.
Page 7: Raimondo de Soncino to the Duke of Milan, in J. E. Olson and E. G. Bourne (eds.), *The Northmen, Columbus and Cabot* (Barnes and Noble, 1959), p. 426.
Page 9: Giovanni da Verrazano to King Francis I, quoted by J. H. Parry, *The European Reconnaissance, Selected Documents* (Macmillan, 1968), pp. 266–77.
Page 15: Sebastian Cabot, *Ordinances*, in Richard Hakluyt, *The Principal Navigations, Voyages, Traffiques and Discoveries of the English Nation* (J. M. Dent, 1927), Vol. one, p. 235.
Page 17: Clement Adam, in Hakluyt, *op. cit.*, p. 271.
Page 19: Giovanni Michiel in Llewelyn Powys, *Henry Hudson* (Bodley Head, 1927), p. 15. Willoughby's diary, quoted by Richard Hakluyt, *op. cit.*, p. 253.
Page 21: Richard Chancellor, *The Book of the Great and Mighty Emperor of Russia*, in Richard Hakluyt, *op. cit.*, pp. 257–58.
Page 23: Quoted by Jeanette Mirsky, *Northern Conquest – The Story of Arctic Exploration* (Hamish Hamilton, 1934), p. 46.
Page 25: George Best, *A True Discourse of the Late Voyage of Discovery for Finding a Passage to Cathay* (1578), in Richard Hakluyt, *op. cit.*, Vol. five, p. 196.
Page 27: Dionyse Settle, *The Second Voyage of Master Martin Frobisher*, in Hakluyt, *op. cit.*, Vol. five, pp. 148–89.
Page 31: George Best, *op. cit.*, p. 218.
Page 32: *Ibid.*, pp. 237–39.
Page 35: *Captain Arthur Barlowe's Narrative*, in Stefan Lorant (ed.), *The New World* (Duell, Sloan and Pearce, 1946), p. 128 and p. 130.
Page 37: Thomas Hariot, *A Brief and True Report of the New Found Land of Virginia* (1588), in Lorant, *op. cit.*, p. 250.
Page 39: *Ibid.*, p. 270.
Page 41: John White, *Report of His Last Voyage to Virginia,* in Lorant, *op. cit.*, p. 175.

CONTENTS

The Search for Cathay

Until the 1400s, Europeans rarely traveled far from home, and they had little knowledge of foreign countries. The stories they heard of distant lands were usually full of wild exaggerations. One country in Asia particularly fascinated them – China, which Europeans then called Cathay. Cathay was thought to be unbelievably rich in gold and precious stones.

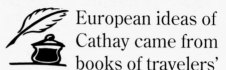 European ideas of Cathay came from books of travelers' tales, such as *The Travels of Sir John Mandeville,* which was written in the late 1300s. This passage describes the cups and bowls used at the ruler of Cathay's table:

All the vessels which are used for serving in his hall are of crystal or fine gold. And all their cups are of emeralds or sapphires or other precious stones.

They make no vessels of silver, for they set no store by silver. They will neither eat nor drink of vessels made of it; they use it for steps, pavements, for halls and chambers.

This flattened-out globe shows the world known to Europeans in the 1400s. Cathay is on the right.

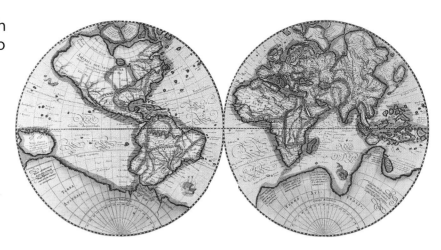

The Europeans' search for a western route to Cathay showed that there was another continent (America) between Europe and Asia. Compare this 1587 map with the one on the opposite page.

In the 1400s, Europeans began to search for new sea routes to Asia, hoping to find the wealth of Cathay. The Portuguese were the first, sailing south and east around the southern tip of Africa.

Then Christopher Columbus, an Italian seafarer, convinced the king and queen of Spain that one could reach Cathay by sailing west, across the Atlantic Ocean. At the time, Europeans had no idea that a vast continent, America, lay on the other side of this sea.

A fifteenth-century woodcut shows Columbus reaching the islands of the Caribbean. He wrongly believed that he had found a short route to the riches of Cathay.

In 1492, Columbus set sail from Spain. After a long voyage west, he reached the islands of the Caribbean. He mistakenly believed that he had arrived in Asia. Even after three more voyages to the Caribbean, Columbus never learned the full truth of where he was.

"New Found Land"

Christopher Columbus had asked King Henry VII of England to pay for his voyage, but the king had refused. When Columbus found land, Henry realized he had made a mistake. In 1496, he was approached by another Italian seafarer, John Cabot. Cabot said that there was a shorter route to Asia than Columbus's, across the north Atlantic. Henry agreed to help him.

In 1497, Cabot sailed west from Bristol in a single tiny ship. After a month at sea, he reached land. There was no sign of gold or precious stones, but the seas were full of cod, which greatly excited the Bristol sailors.

Above Bristol's role as a great sea port was shown on its arms (or shield).

Left English fish stalls were soon selling the Newfoundland cod.

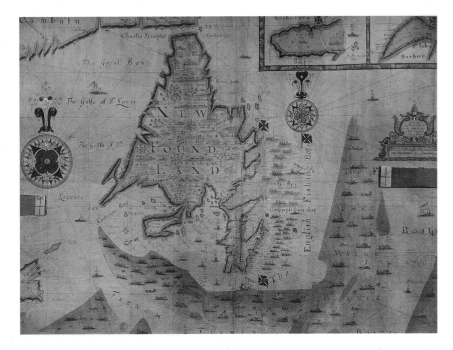

The waters around Newfoundland were swarming with cod. On this map, you can see the English and French fishing fleets that made their way there.

Not knowing the name of the place, the English called it simply "new found land." This eventually became the name of the island Cabot had reached: Newfoundland.

Back in England, Cabot was welcomed as a hero. He set about getting another expedition together, sure that this time he would find the gold of Asia.

In 1498, Cabot set off with five ships. One ship turned back, damaged by a storm. Cabot and the remaining four ships were never heard from

An Italian named Raimondo de Soncino was in London when Cabot returned from his first voyage. He wrote:

This Master John, as a foreigner and a poor man, would not have been believed, had it not been that his companions, who are practically all English and from Bristol, testified that he spoke the truth.

again. It was said that the only lands Cabot had found were on the bottom of the ocean.

The Exploration of the Coast

Columbus and Cabot were both sure that they had found the shortest route to Asia. In fact, they had stumbled upon a vast area of land that no one in Europe even knew existed. It took several more voyages of exploration before Europeans understood this and gave the new land a name: America.

In the 1500s, more and more European ships set sail for the lands found by Columbus and Cabot.

In 1500 and 1501, a Portuguese explorer named Gaspar Corte Real made two voyages across the Atlantic, exploring the coast that lay to the north of Newfoundland. Like Cabot, Corte Real disappeared on his second trip. His brother Miguel sailed off to look for him in 1502, only to vanish himself.

John Cabot's son, Sebastian, explored a long stretch of the coast in 1509. Then, in 1524, Giovanni da Verrazano sailed almost the whole length of the North American coast on behalf of the king of France.

Verrazano made a second voyage in 1528, which ended when he was killed and, it was believed, eaten by people on an island off South America. It was a dangerous business being an explorer of unknown seas and new lands.

This map shows the most important early voyages of exploration to North America – those which revealed the great length of the coast.

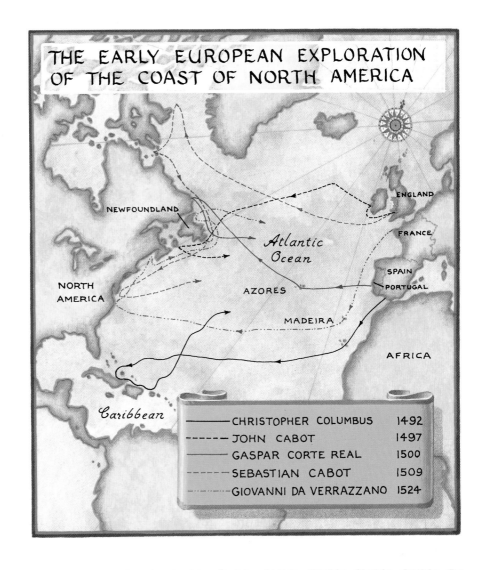

THE EARLY EUROPEAN EXPLORATION OF THE COAST OF NORTH AMERICA

NEWFOUNDLAND

Atlantic Ocean

ENGLAND

FRANCE

SPAIN

PORTUGAL

AZORES

NORTH AMERICA

MADEIRA

AFRICA

Caribbean

—— CHRISTOPHER COLUMBUS	1492	
----- JOHN CABOT	1497	
—— GASPAR CORTE REAL	1500	
----- SEBASTIAN CABOT	1509	
—·— GIOVANNI DA VERRAZZANO	1524	

 After his voyage in 1524, Verrazano reported his findings in a letter to Francis I, the king of France. He wrote:

My intention in this voyage was to reach Cathay and the extreme east of Asia, not expecting to find such an obstacle of new land as I found...

All the ancient writers believed our Western Ocean to be the same as the Eastern Ocean of India, without land in between.... This opinion is now proved to be untrue, for land has been found...

The French in Canada

Europeans were learning about the length of North America from their voyages, but they still had no idea how wide it was. If it was a narrow continent, it might be possible to find a way through it. Then Cathay might still be only a short distance away.

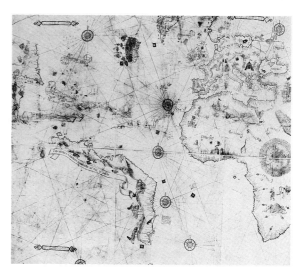

By 1504, when this map was drawn, Europeans were compiling a picture of the east coast of America (center).

Jacques Cartier, explorer of Canada

A French explorer named Jacques Cartier set sailed in 1534 to find a route through North America to Cathay. He reached the coast of what is known today as Canada and explored the mouth of the vast St. Lawrence River. He thought it might be a strait, or passage of water, through America. Cartier made friends with the local people, the Hurons. On a second trip the following year, he sailed up the St. Lawrence River to a place the Hurons called Quebec.

In Quebec, a Huron chief named Donnaconna told Cartier about a wealthy kingdom to the west. It was called Saguenay and was rich in gold and rubies. The people there had white skins and wore woollen clothes, just like the French.

Cartier was very excited by Donnaconna's stories. Unfortunately, they were not true. Donnaconna was eager to please the strangers and so he told them what he thought they wanted to hear. The French believed all the stories, even when they were told of men who could fly. America seemed so strange anyway that they saw no reason to disbelieve Donnaconna.

Forgetting about a route to Cathay, Cartier and other French explorers began to search for Saguenay. They never found it, but, as a result of their explorations, many French people eventually settled in Canada.

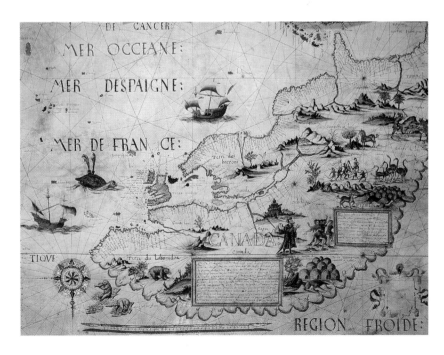

A French map of Canada from 1550, showing the strange animals and people that were thought to live there. This has North at the bottom; you need to turn the book upside down to get the usual view.

A Northern Route to Cathay?

By the 1520s, both the Spanish and the Portuguese were bringing back riches from their voyages of exploration. In 1521, the Spanish conquered the wealthy Aztec empire of Mexico and began to ship back gold from the conquered land, which they called New Spain. At the same time, Spanish ships were finding their way to Asia by sailing southwest, through the Strait of Magellan near the bottom of America, and across the Pacific Ocean.

Meanwhile, the Portuguese had found a southeast route to India, by sailing around the bottom of Africa. Their ships were bringing back large amounts of Indian spices, goods that were rare and very expensive in Europe.

The English watched the Spanish and Portuguese with growing envy. Compared to their wealth, all the English had to show for their voyages was fish. The Bristol fishermen were bringing cod back by the shipload from Newfoundland, the land found by John Cabot.

In 1527, a Bristol merchant named Robert Thorne wrote a letter to King Henry VIII. He argued that one route was left to be explored, in the north.

The bustling Portuguese port of Lisbon grew rich from the spice trade with India.

A View of a Stage, also ye manner of Fishing for, Curing & Drying of Cod at NEW FOUND LAND. A. The Habit of the Fishermen. B. The Line. C The manner of Fishing. D. The Dressers of the Fish. E. The Trough into which they throw the Cod when dressed. F. Salt Boxes. G. The manner of carrying the Cod. H. The Cleansing of the Cod. I. A Press to extract the Oyl from the Cods Liver. K. A Cask to receive the Water and Blood that comes from the Livers. L. another Cask to receive the Oyl. M. The manner of drying the Cod.

Above English fishermen salting and packing cod in Newfoundland.
Below This flattened-out globe shows why the shortest route to Asia appeared to be across the North.

It seemed obvious that there should be a short route to Cathay across the north. You could sail northwest around the top of America, northeast across the top of Europe, or due north over the Arctic.

On a globe, all these routes looked very short compared to the great distances traveled by the Portuguese and Spanish. Nobody in England knew that much of the Arctic was blocked by ice. They had no idea of the terrible weather conditions that sailors would find there.

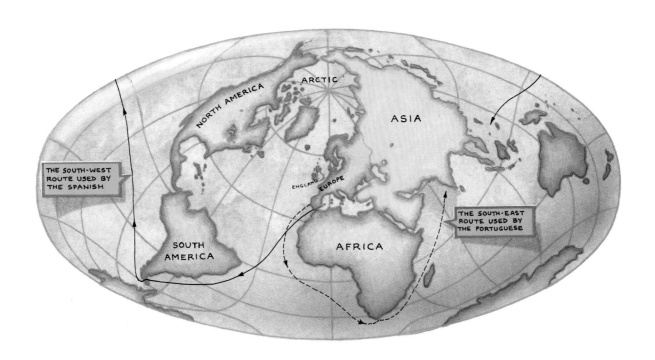

THE SOUTH-WEST ROUTE USED BY THE SPANISH

THE SOUTH-EAST ROUTE USED BY THE PORTUGUESE

ARCTIC
NORTH AMERICA
ASIA
ENGLAND
EUROPE
SOUTH AMERICA
AFRICA

The Merchant Adventurers

In December 1551, a group of London merchants joined together to form the Company of Merchant Adventurers of England for the Discovery of Lands Unknown. This was the first of a series of merchant companies formed to pay for voyages of exploration. Their aim was to find a foreign market for English goods, especially wool.

Each merchant gave a sum of £25. Soon they had raised enough money to buy and equip three ships for a voyage to Cathay. Noblemen, educated

Merchants like these put a lot of money into exploration.

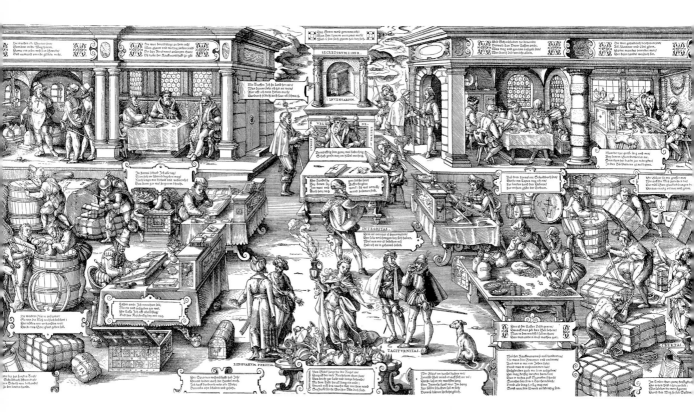

Cabot drew up a list of instructions for the voyage. Like most Christians of the time, Cabot believed that a ship's safety depended on God's good will. Any behavior that upset God could put the whole ship at risk:

No detestable swearing to be used in any ship, nor filthy tales or ungodly talk. This provokes God's most just anger and sword of vengeance...

Sebastian Cabot was an experienced explorer.

men, and experienced sea captains provided advice and leadership. After many discussions, the company decided to try the northeast route to Asia, sailing around the top of Europe.

Sebastian Cabot was made the head of the company. As an experienced explorer, it was his job to plan the route and to give advice on how to lead a voyage. Sir Hugh Willoughby, a handsome courtier and soldier, was chosen to command the ships. He knew nothing about the sea but he would make a good impression on the Emperor of Cathay!

His second in command, Richard Chancellor, was a skilled navigator at sea – he knew how to find his way and direct the course of a ship.

The Ships Set Sail

Willoughby's ships were specially strengthened with lead to protect their sides against the attacks of a worm that was thought to live in the warm seas off China. This shows how carefully the voyage was prepared.

Willoughby's ship, the *Bona Esperanza,* had a crew of thirty-five men. Chancellor sailed with fifty men in the *Edward Bonaventure*. The smallest ship, the *Bona Confidentia*, carried twenty-eight men. Among the crews were cooks, carpenters, gunners, eleven merchants, a surgeon, and a priest.

On May 10, 1553, the three ships set off down the Thames River for the open sea.

The Thames River, drawn in 1616

A writer named Clement Adam described the scene as the ships set sail:

The greater ships were towed down with boats, and oars. The sailors, all dressed in blue, made their way with care. They came to Greenwich, where the Court then lay. Immediately the courtiers came running out, and the common people flocked together, standing very thick upon the shore. At this, the ships fired their cannon in salute.

An English master sailor holding a plumb line

One sailor stood in the poop of the ship and waved farewell to his friends. Another stood in the top of the ship.

At last, with a good wind, they hoisted up sail and gave themselves to the sea, making their last good-bye to their native country, which they did not know whether they should ever return to see again.

Willoughby in Lapland

As they sailed northeast along the coast of Norway, a terrible storm hit the fleet. The ships were scattered by the fierce wind. Willoughby managed to find the *Bona Confidentia*, but he could not find Chancellor's ship. He took his two vessels to the icy coast of Lapland, the weather growing worse all the time. Willoughby decided to spend the winter there and wait for warmer weather.

The following year, the two ships were found. All on board had died of the bitter cold or of scurvy, a disease caused by the lack of fresh food.

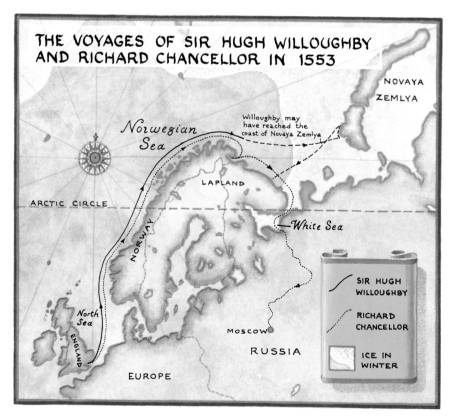

This map shows the routes of Willoughby to Lapland and of Chancellor (his journey is described on page 20). Much of the Arctic Ocean is solid ice all year round. During the winter months, the ice spreads farther south, reaching the coast of Lapland.

Because of the changes in the ice at sea, the Arctic is difficult to map. This is a good sixteenth-century map and shows Norway (Norvegia) and Lapland (Lappia).

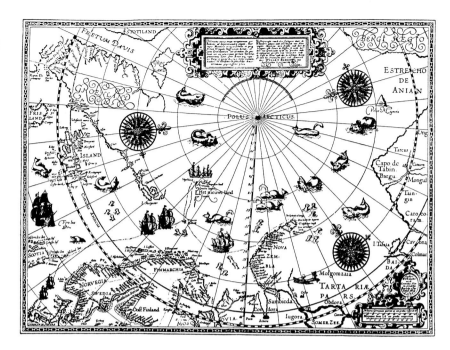

An Italian named Giovanni Michiel was in London when the two ships were brought back to England. He wrote:

The vessels have returned safe, bringing with them the two vessels of the first voyage, having found them with the men on board all frozen... some of them seated in the act of writing, pen still in hand and the paper before them, others at tables, plate in hand and spoon in mouth, and others in various postures, like statues...

Willoughby's diary was found on board. Here is part of the last entry:

After remaining in this harbor a week, seeing the year far spent, and also very evil weather, as frost, snow, and hail, we thought it best to winter there. We sent out three men south-southwest, to search if they could find people. They went three days journey, but could find none. After that, we sent another three westward. They also returned without finding any people.

The Court of Ivan the Terrible

While Willoughby was freezing in Lapland, his second in command, Richard Chancellor, had reached the coast of Russia. Not much was known about this country in western Europe at the time. It was ruled by a famous czar, Ivan IV, nicknamed Ivan the Terrible because of his cruelty.

The English were greeted on the coast by Russians who invited them to Moscow, their capital city. They traveled upriver and by horse-drawn sleigh to the court of the czar.

The Russians must have looked very strange to their visitors. The English had never seen people dressed like this merchant's family.

Richard Chancellor described the banquet held by Ivan the Terrible in honor of his visitors from the West. The czar was also known as the Duke of Muscovy (Muscovy is the old name for Russia).

I came into the dining chamber where the Duke himself sat in a gown of silver, with a crown upon his head... The number that dined there that day was two hundred, and all were served in golden vessels...

Before the food was served, the Duke sent to every man a great piece of bread, and the bearer called the person so sent to by his name aloud, and said, "John Vasilievich Emperor of Russia and great Duke of Muscovy doth reward thee with bread."

Also, before dinner, he changed his crown, and during dinner he wore two crowns, so that I saw three different crowns on his head in one day.

Ivan the Terrible was a cruel man who killed his own son in a fit of anger. Luckily, Chancellor and his men never saw this side of Ivan.

The visit marked the start of a new trade between England and Russia. English merchants would carry guns and woollen cloth to be traded for Russian furs and tallow (animal fat that was used for candles).

Chancellor may not have found Cathay, but his voyage had not been a failure.

The Dutch in the Arctic

The Dutch were also searching for a northeast route to Cathay through the Arctic.

The most famous Dutch explorer was Willem Barents, who made three trips to the north. On his third voyage, in 1596, he rounded Novaya Zemlya, a group of islands off the northern coast of Russia, and sailed into the icy Kara Sea. Here the ice closed in on the ship, squeezing and

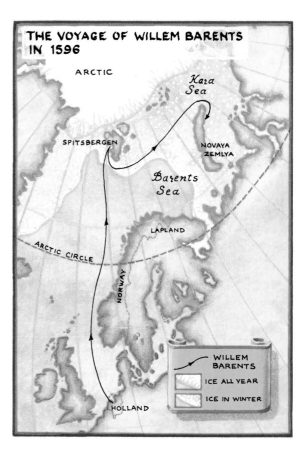

Barents's ship stuck fast in the Arctic ice. The men killed polar bears and used their fat to light oil lamps.

crushing it. According to one of the crew, the sight and sound of the splitting ship made all the hairs on their heads stand upright with fear.

They were forced to abandon the ship and cross the ice to Novaya Zemlya.

Here the Dutchmen spent the long, dark winter in a shelter built out of driftwood. They killed polar bears, using their fat to light oil lamps. By January, they were beginning to suffer from scurvy.

When the warmer weather arrived, they set off in the ship's tiny lifeboats. Barents and one of his men died on the way back. The rest reached the coast of Lapland, from where they got home safely.

Barents is still remembered in the name of the sea to the west of Novaya Zemlya, the Barents Sea.

 Gerrit de Vere, one of Barents's crew, described the cold of the shelter:

It was so extremely cold that the fire cast almost no heat; for, as we put our feet to the fire, we burned our hose [stockings or socks] *before we could feel the heat. And what is more, if we had not sooner smelled them than felt them, we should have burned them completely away before we knew it.*

Barents and his men did their best to keep warm in their wooden shelter during the long, dark winter. In the Arctic, there is no sun from November 3 to January 24.

23

Martin Frobisher

By the 1570s, English hopes for a route to Cathay had switched to the northwest. Sir Humphrey Gilbert wrote a book in which he argued that a northwest passage could be found much farther south than the icy northeast route.

Gilbert raised the money to try out his idea. The man he chose to lead his planned voyage of exploration was an ex-pirate named Martin Frobisher.

Above Sir Humphrey Gilbert proposed a northwest route to Cathay.
Below Frobisher's route took him to Baffin Island.

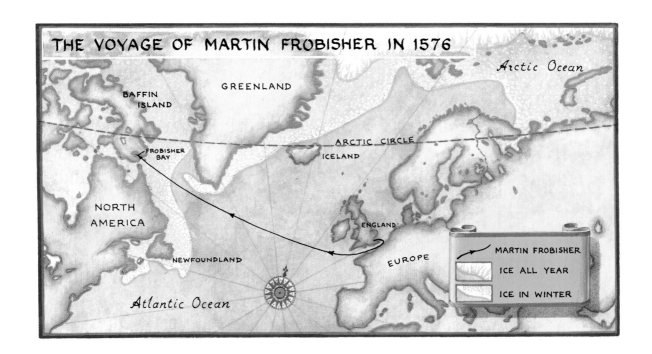

THE VOYAGE OF MARTIN FROBISHER IN 1576

Arctic Ocean

GREENLAND

BAFFIN ISLAND

FROBISHER BAY

ARCTIC CIRCLE

ICELAND

NORTH AMERICA

ENGLAND

NEWFOUNDLAND

EUROPE

Atlantic Ocean

MARTIN FROBISHER
ICE ALL YEAR
ICE IN WINTER

Frobisher was sure that he had found a clear way through North America to Cathay. You can see it marked on this map, which was drawn after his first voyage.

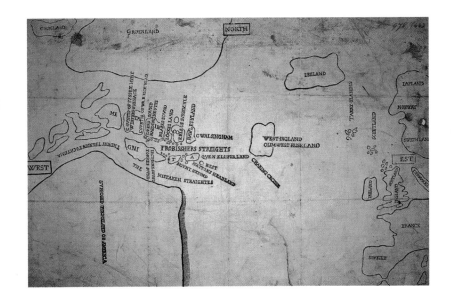

In June 1576, Frobisher sailed from the Thames with three ships. In fierce weather, one of the ships sank. Off Greenland, the crew of the second ship decided to sail home – they could see that the northwest was just as cold as the northeast.

Frobisher sailed on alone and reached Baffin Island, where he believed he had found the strait leading to Cathay. He called it Frobisher's Strait. In fact, it was only a bay, a dead end, known today as Frobisher Bay.

There he saw a strange sight ahead of him.

George Best, who sailed with Frobisher on a later voyage, described what the explorer saw off Baffin Island:

He saw a number of small things fleeting in the sea far off, which he supposed to be porpoises or seals, or some kind of strange fishes; but coming nearer, he discovered them to be men in small boats made of leather…. He had several meetings with them, and they came aboard his ship, and brought him salmon and raw flesh and fish, and greedily devoured the same before our men's faces.

The Inuit

Above One of the first European drawings of Inuit mistakenly shows them hunting on skis. The Inuit did not use skis at this time.

Below This later drawing is much more accurate. It shows that the Inuit wore fur clothes.

The strange men that Frobisher met called themselves the Inuit, meaning "people," and they called their leather boats kayaks. Today, these people are often known as Eskimos, which means "eaters of raw meat." This was what the peoples who lived to the south of the Inuit called them.

The English sailors thought the Inuit were simple savages.

Yet they knew how to survive in one of the coldest and harshest places on earth. The Inuit lived by hunting and fishing. Animals such as seals supplied all their needs. Skins were used for clothes, tents, and boats. The Inuit also trained dogs called huskies to pull their sleds when they traveled overland.

Their life was so well suited to the icy climate that it hardly changed over the years. Three hundred years after Frobisher's voyage, the Inuit were still living in very much the same way.

 Dionyse Settle, who sailed with Frobisher on his second voyage to Baffin Island, described the Inuit way of life. It seemed very strange to the explorers:
They eat their meat all raw. For lack of water, they will eat ice, as pleasantly as we will eat sugar candy...

They keep certain dogs not much unlike wolves, which they yoke together, as we do horses, to a sled. And when the dogs are no longer fit for this, they eat them ...

Those beasts, fishes, and birds that they kill are their meat, drink, clothing, houses, bedding, shoes, thread and sails for their boats, and almost all their riches.

This is another early picture, showing Inuit hunting seals on the Arctic ice.

Five Men Lost

Five Englishmen went ashore to trade with the Inuit and disappeared. Frobisher was desperate to get them back. He decided to capture an Inuit man to swap for them. He drew one to the ship's side by

A later attack on Frobisher's men by the usually friendly Inuit

holding out a bell and ringing it. When a man paddled up in a kayak, Frobisher pulled him on board, still in his boat.

Even though Frobisher had captured the Inuit, he could not get his own men back. They were never seen again.

Frobisher eventually gave up and sailed home, bringing with him the strange man and his boat. The Inuit caused a great stir back in London, though he died soon after from a cold.

Even more sensational was a piece of black rock that Frobisher had found on Baffin Island. Experts in London said that it contained gold. It seemed that the English would not have to find Cathay after all. There was enormous wealth to be had much closer to home.

This portrait of Martin Frobisher was painted on his return to England. He was given a hero's welcome.

The mystery of what happened to the five Englishmen who vanished was finally explained three hundred years later.

In 1862, an American explorer named Charles Hall met an old Inuit woman who told him a story. She said that long ago, "kodlunas," or white men, had come to their land. Five "kodlunas" had been captured by the Inuit. After a while, the Inuit let them go, and they built a boat with wood left behind by Frobisher. They sailed away and disappeared.

In 1862, the island where they made their boat was still called Kodlunarn, or "white man's island," by the Inuit.

Mining for Gold

In 1577, Frobisher sailed back to Baffin Island with three ships. This time, he was after gold. The search for Cathay was almost forgotten.

Frobisher spent a month mining and collected 200 tons of the black rock. He also captured an Inuit man and a woman with a young baby. Then he set sail for England.

Back in England, the Inuit man gave a display of duck hunting in his kayak on the Avon River. He was also introduced to Queen Elizabeth I. She was so impressed by him that she gave him permission to hunt swans on the Thames. After a month in England the Inuit died, just like the first captive.

This woodcut shows the captured Inuit man hunting seabirds. The woman and her baby are in the background.

The captured Inuit posed for these portraits by the English artist John White. The baby peeps out from the mother's hood.

 George Best, Frobisher's second in command, described what happened when the captured Inuit man and woman were brought together for the first time:

At their first meeting, they looked at each other very sadly for a long time, without saying anything, as if their grief had taken away their power of speech. Then the woman suddenly looked away and began to sing, as if she was thinking of another matter.

Being brought together again, the man broke the silence first, and with a serious face began to tell a long solemn tale to the woman, who listened closely to him.

Afterward, having grown to know each other better, they were left together, so that I think the one would hardly have lived without the comfort of the other.

Fool's Gold

In 1578, Frobisher made a third voyage with a great fleet of fifteen ships. This was paid for by some of the richest people in England. They had joined a new Company of Cathay, hoping to share in the gold found by Frobisher.

Among the crews were thirty Cornish tin miners, most of them "pressed," or forced to join the crews against their will.

 George Best described the dangers of the ice:

We were forced many times to strike great rocks of ice, and so as it were make way through mighty mountains.... It is worth noting how the mariners and poor miners (unused to such hardships) overcame these great dangers. With poles and pieces of timber, they stood almost day and night without any rest, bearing off the force of the ice. Otherwise, it would have stricken through the sides of their ships.

Huge icebergs like these could crush a wooden ship.

This eighteenth-century drawing shows Frobisher's great fleet at Baffin Island, with the miners making and mending their tools.

This was a common method of getting people to crew ships in the sixteenth century.

It was a terribly cold summer and Frobisher's Strait was almost blocked by ice. The ships lost sight of each other in thick fog, and one of them sank in a fierce storm.

After reaching Baffin Island, the miners spent a month gathering the black rocks, in conditions of great hardship.

A lump of fool's gold

When winter came, the ships sailed home carrying over one thousand tons of rock.

Bad news was waiting for Frobisher in England. The black rocks were not gold at all, but worthless iron pyrites known as "fool's gold."

The Company of Cathay lost all its money and Frobisher was in disgrace. The black rocks ended up being used to mend roads.

The Idea of a Colony

After the failure of Frobisher's mining venture, the English came up with another plan for making their country rich. The man behind it was Sir Walter Raleigh, half-brother of Sir Humphrey Gilbert.

Raleigh's plan was to found an English colony, or settlement, on the east coast of America. The settlers could work there, growing crops such as sugar cane and bananas that could not grow in the cooler English climate. These crops could then be traded for English wool. The important thing was to find somewhere with a good climate, fertile soil, and friendly local people.

In 1584, Raleigh sent two Englishmen, Philip Amadas and Arthur Barlowe, to find a suitable place for his colony. They sailed first to the

As well as organizing voyages of exploration, Sir Walter Raleigh was a poet, scientist, and soldier.

Caribbean, and then traveled north up the coast of America until they arrived at an island called Roanoke.

On Roanoke, the English were delighted to find thick woods, good soil, and

Arthur Barlowe described the welcome he received from one of the Algonquins:

He made signs of joy and welcome, first striking his own head and breast and then ours, smiling and trying to show that we were all brothers, all made of the same flesh. He then made a long speech, and we presented him with gifts...

We were given everything they could provide. We found these people gentle, loving, and faithful, lacking all cunning and trickery.

welcoming people. These people were Algonquins, who lived across a large area of eastern North America. They seemed to say that their land was called "Wingandacoa." In fact, they were saying, "You wear fine clothes!"

This map by John White shows the coast visited by Raleigh's ships, with Roanoke near the top. Raleigh's coat of arms is painted with the land's new English name, Virginia.

The Algonquins

The woods on the east coast of North America were full of game such as deer, which the Algonquins hunted with bows and arrows. They were also expert at fishing from boats carved out of tree trunks. They built fish weirs – barriers of stakes that were stuck in the riverbeds. The Algonquins then drove schools of fish toward the weirs, where they would be trapped by the stakes and could be speared easily.

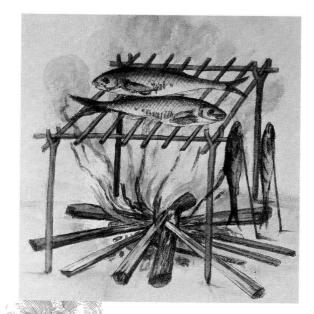

Above John White painted many scenes of Algonquin life. This shows herrings being cooked.

Left Men using fire to hollow out a canoe. This was copied from one of White's paintings.

36

Thomas Hariot, who visited Roanoke in 1585, described the Algonquins' fishing methods:

As they have neither steel nor iron, they fasten to reeds or long rods the sharp hollow tail of a certain fish, something like a sea crab, and with this they spear fish both day and night... They have different kinds of fish, many of them never found in our waters, and all of an excellent taste.

It is a pleasing sight to see these people wading and sailing in their rivers. They are free from the care of heaping up riches for their children, content with their present state. They live in friendship with each other, sharing all those things with which God has so bountifully provided them. Yet they do not render Him the thanks which He deserves. So savage is this people, and deprived of the true knowledge of God.

Algonquins fishing in a shallow river using fish weirs, canoes, and spears

As well as hunting and fishing, the Algonquins were farmers. The women grew corn, squashes, and different kinds of beans in fields close to their villages. At the time, these crops were all unknown to the English.

37

Virginia

In 1585, Sir Walter Raleigh sent a new expedition of seven ships to "Wingandacoa," now renamed Virginia. On board were 108 colonists – people who were setting out to make a new life in America.

The English landed, again, on Roanoke Island. The friendly Algonquins brought them food and showed the English where they could build their settlement.

Unfortunately, the friendship between the English and the Algonquins did not last. The problem was that the English expected the Algonquins to do all their work. They never learned to fish for themselves – the Algonquins built fish weirs for the English, who could not

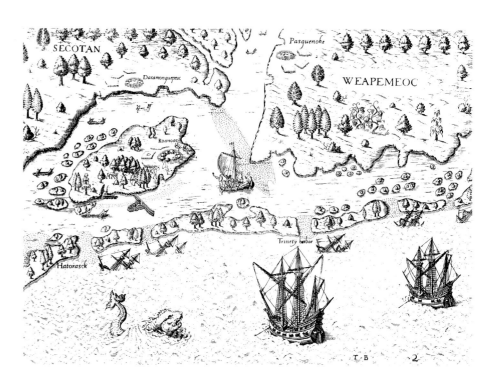

English ships arriving at Roanoke. You can see the Algonquin villages, fish weirs, and canoes.

Thomas Hariot described the effect that the English first had on the Algonquins:

They marveled at all that we had, such as compasses, magnets, fireworks, guns, books, and clocks that seemed to go by themselves. All these things were beyond their understanding, just as reading and writing were completely strange to them. They thought all these things must have been made by the gods...

One time, their corn began to wither because of an unusual drought. They feared that this had happened because they had displeased us in some way. A few of them came to us asking that we should pray to our English god that he should preserve their corn.

The Algonquin children loved the little wooden dolls that the English had brought with them as presents.

even repair them. The settlers' cattle and pigs badly damaged the Algonquins' cornfields.

In 1585, the Algonquins rose against the English. The colony was soon under siege. Just in time, an English fleet arrived, commanded by Sir Francis Drake. He took the colonists home to England.

The Second Settlement

In 1587, the English made a second attempt at settling in America. John White, the official artist of the first settlement, was made governor of the new colony. Among the 150 settlers who made the voyage across the Atlantic were seventeen women and nine children.

Three weeks after their arrival, one of the Englishmen was killed by the Algonquins, who had not forgotten the behavior of the earlier settlers. John White tried to arrange a meeting to restore their friendship with the Algonquins, but they did not come. Furious, White attacked a local village.

An Algonquin ruler seen from the front and the back. The Algonquins were not pleased to see the English back in their land, and they attacked them with the bows and arrows they used for hunting.

John White's painting of an Algonquin village, showing the houses they lived in, the fields where they grew corn, and a religious dance

 John White described his return to the colony in 1590:

We hailed the shore with friendly greetings but got no answer. At daybreak we landed and proceeded to walk along the shore until we came to the place where I had left our colony in the year 1587...

We discovered that their dwellings had been torn down and that a strong enclosure with a high palisade [barrier] *of huge trees had been built.... We entered the palisade, where we found some iron bars, cannon shot, and other heavy things overgrown with weeds. From there we went to the beach, hoping to come upon some of the settlers, or their boats. But there was no sign of them.*

White then sailed back to England to get fresh supplies for his colony. He was unable to return for four years because England was at war with Spain. Ships could not be spared to sail to the colony.

In 1590, White returned to find that every member of the colony had vanished. To this day, nobody knows what happened to them.

Jamestown

Despite the repeated failures, the English did not give up their dream of making a settlement in America. A Company of Virginia was formed to raise money and attract people who would be willing to try living in the new land. The Company's advertisements painted a glowing picture of America.

The site chosen for the colony was Chesapeake Bay, some distance north of Roanoke. In 1607 a new town was founded there, called Jamestown after King James I. Unlike the earlier settlements, Jamestown succeeded.

Above John Smith, a tough explorer and the leader of the Jamestown settlement

Left Smith had many adventures while exploring Virginia. Here, he is pictured being captured by Algonquins.

42

Smith spent a month as a prisoner of the Algonquins and was then set free to continue exploring. Thanks to his journeys, the English were able to make this map of Virginia.

At first, the English had no idea of how to survive. Instead of growing crops, they lived off their supplies, which lasted five months. Like the earlier settlers, they expected the Algonquins to take care of them but ended up fighting them. They suffered from diseases such as malaria, caused by the strange climate. In the first year, two-thirds of the 105 settlers died of starvation, disease, or Algonquin attacks.

John Smith, who became leader of the colony, forced the English to work. He ordered that those who did not work would not be fed. Unlike the earlier settlements, Jamestown was helped by the arrival of new settlers and supplies. The Company of Virginia also made sure that Jamestown had enough money to keep it going until it produced a profit. This happened when the settlers at last found something they could sell back in England – tobacco. Many English people disapproved of smoking as a strange foreign habit, but the money it brought in saved the Jamestown colony.

The Early Settlers

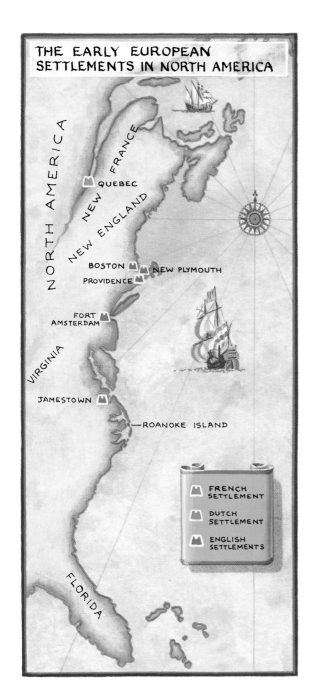

THE EARLY EUROPEAN SETTLEMENTS IN NORTH AMERICA

NORTH AMERICA

NEW FRANCE

QUEBEC

NEW ENGLAND

BOSTON

PROVIDENCE

NEW PLYMOUTH

FORT AMSTERDAM

VIRGINIA

JAMESTOWN

ROANOKE ISLAND

FLORIDA

FRENCH SETTLEMENT

DUTCH SETTLEMENT

ENGLISH SETTLEMENTS

Jamestown was only the first of the successful settlements of North America. In 1608, the French returned to Quebec, where they founded their own settlement. Like the Jamestown people, the French settlers found products to sell back in Europe – animal furs rather than tobacco.

In 1620, a very different type of settlement was set up in Massachusetts, by English people who had arrived on a ship called the *Mayflower*. They called their new home, Plymouth – the early settlers often named places in America after towns they had left back home. Today, we remember the Plymouth settlers as the Pilgrim Fathers. They are still celebrated every year in America on Thanksgiving Day.

The Pilgrims had religious reasons for going to America.

They hated the elaborate ceremonies of the official Church in England and they wanted to set up their own Church. They did not have as much money as Jamestown, but they were hard-working farming people and they were joined by fresh arrivals of Christians who shared their views.

Smallpox, brought to America by the Europeans, had a terrible effect on the native peoples.

All along the east coast of America, European-style towns were built: places such as Boston (in 1630) and Providence (in 1636). In 1626, the Dutch founded their own settlement, Fort Amsterdam, which later became New York. It was the start of a new nation.

Life was very hard for the first settlers. They had to learn to live in a strange land and grow unfamiliar crops. There was always the risk of attacks by the Algonkins and other native peoples. Gradually, the Algonkins were pushed back from the coast – their bows and arrows were not much use against English guns. They also died in huge numbers from European diseases, such as smallpox.

An early picture of the Dutch settlement, Fort Amsterdam. The island is now part of New York.

45

GLOSSARY

Algonquin The name of many different peoples who lived in the east of North America in the sixteenth century. They all shared the same Algonquin language.

Arctic The northernmost part of the earth. It is a bitterly cold area where much of the sea is always frozen.

Bay Where a coast curves inward.

Caribbean The sea and a group of islands off the east coast of Central America.

Cathay An old European name for China.

Climate The usual weather of an area.

Continent A large area of land – Europe, Africa, and North and South America are all continents.

Courtier A person who is part of the group of advisers and other people around a ruler.

Czar The title of the ruler of Russia. It comes from the ancient Roman ruler's title, Caesar.

Detestable Hated.

Eskimo The name given to the Inuit by the people who lived to the south of them. It means "eaters of raw meat." Many Inuit, especially those in North America, do not like this name.

Huron A native people of eastern North America. They lived beside the St. Lawrence River where they hunted and fished. They made friends with the first French explorers.

Inuit The people who live in the Arctic, from Alaska to Greenland.

Malaria A disease spread by mosquitoes.

Merchant A person who trades large amounts of goods, especially with other countries.

Northwest passage A sea route from Europe to Asia across the north of America. Europeans searched for a northwest passage for hundreds of years, hoping to use it as a trade route. As recently as 1845, two English ships were lost in the attempt. The way through was finally found in 1903–1906 by a Norwegian explorer named Roald Amundsen.

Plumb line A line weighted with lead. Sailors held the line over the ship's side to test the depth of the water.

Porpoise A small whale.

Scurvy A disease caused by the lack of vitamin C from fresh fruit and vegetables. It was common among early sailors.

Seafarer A sailor.

Settlement A place where people from another country or place set up a new life.

Smallpox A disease brought to America by the Europeans. The native people had no resistance to European diseases, and they died by the millions.

Weir A fence set in a waterway for catching fish.

BOOKS TO READ

Alexander, Brian and Cherry Alexander. *Inuit.* Austin: Raintree Steck-Vaughn, 1992.

Bullen, Susan. *The Arctic and Its People.* People and Places. New York: Thomson Learning, 1994.

Chrisp, Peter. *Voyages to the New World.* Exploration & Encounters. New York: Thomson Learning, 1993.

Humble, Richard. *The Voyages of Columbus.* Exploration Through the Ages. New York: Franklin Watts, 1991.

Matthews, Rupert. *Explorer.* New York: Alfred A. Knopf Books for Young Readers, 1991.

Reische, Diana. *Founding the American Colonies.* First Books. New York: Franklin Watts, 1989.

Waterlow, Julia, *The Explorer Through History.* Journey Through History. New York: Thomson Learning, 1994.

INDEX